T0116519

PEACEFULNESS EXISTS

OMARI GREY

authorHOUSE®

AuthorHouse™
1663 Liberty Drive
Bloomington, IN 47403
www.authorhouse.com
Phone: 833-262-8899

Published by AuthorHouse   04/26/2023

ISBN: 979-8-8230-0727-6 (sc)
ISBN: 979-8-8230-0726-9 (e)

Print information available on the last page.

This book is printed on acid-free paper.

CONTENTS

PREFACE

I began writing this book after suffering from a traumatic brain injury caused by a head-on collision. The physical state of my body was not only significantly different, but I also dealt with headaches, body pain, and loss of speech and eyesight. On a scale from 1 to 10, as a human being, I became a ZERO! This life experience has truly humbled me.

My brain injury even made it difficult for me to sleep. When everyone in my family slept, I would write my book in the stillness of the night. I sat wheelchair-bound on my deck during the spring and summer months, watching my four boys become young men. In some ways, my car accident benefited them as they had to take over much of the business responsibilities of our farm. The boys would organize the barn and participate in the process of raising our animals, from feeding and delivering meat to our clients. They gained hands-on experience in being competent business people. My sons focused on their school work while embracing becoming intellectually stimulated entrepreneurial farming individuals.

My five daughters also gained additional responsibilities in the home, assisting with cooking and meal preparation, along with their school work. Since I was a math teacher, I began instructing them on mathematics using candy as a reward. I was extremely busy before my accident, pursuing entrepreneurial endeavors and working in three different occupations. According to my wife, I would rarely have time to teach my own kids. My wife said, *"Omari...Thank God for your accident! Now you can help me homeschool our kids and spend time with us."* Whenever the girls saw me, I would ask them addition, subtraction, multiplication, or division problems out loud and force them to solve them mentally. My wife, Apryl-Sakinah McDowell, was extremely busy with our farm business. She had to homeschool our nine kids, run our farm business, tend to the farm operations, and organize our farm workshops.

I would try to assist my wife with these responsibilities, but managing my physical and mental state was an uphill battle. After my traumatic car accident, I would go twice per week to three therapists and participate in Zoom calls with other people with brain injuries. Since I was not working, I had ample time to write my book as a source of reflection and healing. Living on a 2-acre tranquil farm allowed for deep contemplation, aiding my ability to write this book confidently as if this was God's intention. Over time I have lived in three Middle Eastern countries, grew up in two north and south U.S. states, and became close friends with people of diverse backgrounds and nationalities. My life has been extremely enriched by various characters and personalities I have met across the globe.

Pondering on my deck outside of my room, I realized that our lives are similar to the interconnectedness of farm animals. Every different animal – cows, chickens, goats, ducks, dogs, cats, or fish – has their own natural responsibilities. Animals work together to create the richness of our farm. For example, having a dog protects our animals from coyotes or other wild animals. Our chickens eat the worms that would damage the beautiful plants we grow for nutrition. Also, the goats and cows would release some manure, which my boys hated to clean up and organize daily. But that manure strengthened the soil quality for the fruits and vegetables we grew. Human beings are just like farm animals.

Our existence as humans on this planet is a scaled version of the interconnectedness of the farm. The differences in roles and contributions of each animal and planet create a harmonious balance that allows our farm life to continue. This is the premise of my book: the diversity in our differences (race, gender, religion, experiences, and nationality) allows for a better community, company, or organization. It's time to foster our commonalities despite our differences so, just like a farm, we can live a life with peace and tranquility.

After my traumatic brain injury weakened me, I realized that many people deal with societal weaknesses and sometimes worse situations. Our job as fellow humans is to help each other become more aligned with successful human growth. We must understand that God is always watching us.

PART I

Youth, Basketball, and Resiliency

CHAPTER 1

At the age of ten, I was a typical American kid with a mother who worked at school and a father who was a police officer. My experiences up to that point were exceptionally normal - a standard New York kid life. As a small child, I would endlessly play basketball as my main sport and concentrate on excelling in my school work until the sun went down. A child's dorky dream, mixed with education pressure and sports adrenaline, made my life complete. My father worked for the New York City police department. Often, I would accompany him and tag along during his second job of delivering mail to people's houses. Also, I would visit my father's video store near my home; inside his store were childhood video games. I was intrigued by my Nintendo entertainment system.

Our Long Island, New York home had bedrooms for me, my brother, and my parents. It had a nice outside garden where my brother and I would mow the lawn in the summer, and in the fall, we would rake the leaves and put them in plastic bags. We also had a huge basement and a comfortable living room for visiting people. Growing up, I would go to Queens to visit my cousin Kali, my Aunt Dale's daughter. My Aunt Dale graciously helped her younger cousin's children, Roberta and Shaminay, whom I often saw during my visit to Queens. On numerous occasions, I visited nearby Freeport in Long Island to see my Uncle Milton and his kids: Beau, Milty, Mathew, and Aja. Later my Uncle Milton remarried Sheila, who had two more children - Jason and Avi. A strong family bond was important to my mother, so we continued to spend time with them each week.

As a parent reflecting back on my days growing up in the city, I would not allow my children on any of the blocks I frequented in the city during my youth. But as a young child, this was my standard routine. City life was exciting and thrilling to me. Even though my close city neighborhoods were rough, my family didn't have to worry. We were pictured as an ideal family and lived in a safe environment alongside famous celebrities and successful Manhattan businesspeople. In Long Island, NY, I often went to two friends' houses who lived nearby, listened to hip-hop music, played sports at the park, and goofed around for fun. Our family life was a standard upper-middle-class, including kids playing sports and excelling in school. My mother was a school principal and president of an African-American organization; my father was a police officer and business entrepreneur. We lived two miles away from a local park where many of us played lots of basketball for fun.

I often attended basketball games in the city to experience major talents in the sport I loved, accompanied by my Uncle Milton and my brother, Jamel Grey. We would participate in Five Star basketball camps in the summer every year, with many players from top Division I college scholarships ready to practice hardcore basketball. My Uncle Milton was an amazing basketball player; he taught his nephews, my brother, and me how to excel in basketball. My Uncle Milton knew the owner of the Five Star basketball camp, Howard Garfinkel, so getting into the camp was a normal summer event in my youth.

Many of my friends also took a keen interest in basketball throughout their childhoods. I would go to my close friend's house, Jamel Smiley, to play around in our neighborhood block. We would joke around and play basketball or video games—the typical American young kid experience. Sometimes we would go to the nearby park or to his school to play basketball. I would say: *"What's good, Smiley? Are you ready to shoot hoops?"* He commented: *"Hold on, O. Just keep your voice down and don't wake up, my Grandma. Let me get dressed, and then we could go."* Unfortunately, due to his mother passing away, his father stepped up to take care of his children, and they moved into their grandmother's house, which was in our Lake view neighborhood in Long Island, NY. Jamel lived with his older brother, Jamar, who was close to my brother's age. Two Black boys living on the same Long Island street block, one year apart from us in age, and loving basketball, set the reason we were close friends as young children.

Basketball encompassed my life in many ways; everything was focused on improving and becoming a successful basketball player. I was an eager fan who would go to Rutgers Park in Harlem, NY. I often went to the nearby park to play basketball with my older brother, Jamel, or played by myself. It was a customary sports event we used to do. Playing sports in elementary school and constantly perfecting my basketball talent gave me great balance and energy. Part of our responsibilities as parents is to raise our children with *character equilibrium.* Having them involved in activities that build their self-esteem and self-worth and also exude energy is paramount. For Omari Grey, it was the sport of basketball.

KNIFE FIGHT

Early one morning, I woke up and decided to play basketball at the park. I was afraid of the nearby dogs that might get loose, so I sped up my bicycle each time as if I was in an intense bike race. I made it safely to the park, unaware of the dangerous situation that was about to unfold. Playing basketball at the park was a way to improve my sports conditioning as I played against older, more physical players. All of a sudden, during an intense full-court game, I heard a loud argument erupt. As the arguing increased, a crowd began gathering around two guys I grew up with. I foolishly chose to walk towards the mayhem as my curiosity peaked.

This Long Island park was typically calm and serene. But on this day, the men who were arguing escalated their disagreement and began attacking each other with knives. The situation intensified as they attempted to kill each other. Everyone around them watched as if this was normal. I believe they were involved with the drug epidemic in New York, and the argument was over money and drugs. Fights were a common part of city life, so I was not completely shocked by this behavior. It helped me understand why I needed to exercise and work out to increase my body strength in case this situation happened to me. Watching two angry men forcefully lunge at each other with box cutters in their hands convinced me to take this strength training seriously. As I reflect, although my passion was playing basketball, exercising sports, and lifting weights regularly, physical training was my form of self-defense. I was a child focused on playing hard basketball and enhancing my learning skills to go to college. I didn't want my future to have anything to do with men trying to kill each other over drugs.

Overall my years as a youth were not filled with negativity and stress, but rather a great upbringing of a fruitful and constructive life. Some traumatic instances may happen in life that can shape or break you. I chose to allow this incident to make me tougher instead of lowering my character or morale. Instead of blaming traumatic events that took place in a young kid's life as a reason I disrupt, disturb people, or assault individual rights, I reframed it as growing positivity and a strong mindset. All in all, when I think about my youth, it was balanced and stable with some dramatic events. This knife fight I saw challenged me to be stronger physically, mentally, and spiritually. As I reflect as an adult, I believe disruption can offset your comfort, make you work hard, and help you appreciate a fulfilling, successful life.

ORIGINAL BLACK LIVES MATTER

As a youngster, I wanted to act and look cool, so I did my best to relay a chill front. As I approached some neighbors, they would say: *"What's up, 'Little Mel'? How are you doing, little man?"* My community saw me as a younger version of my older brother, Jamel. He was known as an excellent star athlete and would always go to people's parties and events.

There was real love in our neighborhood, and the whole community idealized my mother, Sandra Grey. Starting with an English teaching career, she quickly advanced to a principal position. She was extremely busy with her family, running a school, and being involved in community activism, so she constantly moved around. She also made sure my school career was set up for success by assuring I was in advanced classes in elementary and middle schools. Due to my mother, I was in classes with the smartest children and best teachers.

My mother grew up in Queens, NY, and attended an H.B.C.U. (historically black college/university) – coincidentally, just like my wife's college. We used to live in a pretty secure environment, but it was near cities with a lot of drama and trouble with people of color being treated unfairly. She became the president of the N.A.A.C.P. (National Association for the Advancement of Colored People), an organization that works to protect African-Americans and their Constitutional[1] rights. The N.A.A.C.P. was started by successful African-Americans such as W.E.B. Dubois and Mary Eliza Church and worked to eliminate any form of racial presence in the United States. The New York community viewed my mother as a leader because she would serve them and speak about the ill-treatment of African-Americans in the best eloquent way possible. My mother's ancestors started their lives in America in the shackles of slavery. Her focus was curing the disease of racism towards people of color and increasing equality. Her center of attention was community-building, which I have tried to embrace as her courageous actions inspire me. My mother has always been my role model.

Historically, I am the descendant of enslaved people. My mother's great-grandmother lived in South Carolina and was impregnated with twenty kids due to encounters of rape with slave owners. Enslaving Africans and shipping them to America was very prevalent in the southern U.S. states, and it lasted for centuries. Although slavery was eventually abolished, the terrible slavery time frame only ended approximately a hundred years ago. According to my mother, her light skin is a result of having the D.N.A. of white slave owners due to rape.

My grandfather was a mixed Native American. The Native American community has also faced oppression. They were kidnapped and enslaved by Christopher Columbus, who happened to find America after the Native Americans occupied this land. In American history books, we have viewed Christopher Columbus as a land-discovering European hero and put his face on U.S. dollars. This is such a regressive

---

[1] The Constitution was created by George Washington, who began enslaving people but found that this way of living needed to stop; he then created this law amendment to protect civil liberties to a secure fundamental system of America regardless of racial background.

philosophy, as he helped destroy Native American communities in their own home country. Ironic.

In the 1980s, Michael Griffin was a 23-year-old Black man who lost his life due to a racially motivated event in Howard Beach, in Queens. Michael heard some racial slurs and began fighting a mob of white men and later died after getting hit by their car. The father of one of these men was a protected N.Y.P.D. officer. According to the city mayor, this was the *"number one case in the country."* In addition to this tragedy, three other racially motivated events took place where Black men were killed by white mobs in the 1980s. Racism has a strong hold on the American population and traps people in an inhumane mental box. White Americans have to forcefully unplug and see others as human beings just like themselves. They must rid themselves of tension or fear from the subconscious slavery-existing mind fallacy.

The New York Times wrote an article titled "Black Man Dies After Beach Beating by White in Queens." Many white Americans now understand the struggles of people of color, but we are still fighting white supremacy in many different areas. As a young child, I attended an N.A.A.C.P. protest march in which members said, *"Howard Beach have you heard? This is not Johannesburg!"* White people also spoke this chant aloud, supporting their Black people being wronged and killed unjustly. There were also white Americans in opposition to the protest; they yelled curse words in anger because they felt this event was unnecessary, adding to hostility between opposing sides. My mother took us to the protest to ensure my brother and I stood up for our people's human rights and dignity.

As we continue to hear about the tragic loss of Black lives, we know that racial inequality still exists. It must be conquered with love and affection towards different national, religious, gender, and 'colored' people.

NY TEEN MURDER

I grew up in a diverse community that was primarily Black, and I used to visit Manhattan, Brooklyn, and Queens for excitement. As a young kid, I idolized the rappers I saw and tried to copy their style and persona foolishly. I stood my ground around others, but I could not fool my mother. My brother and I were invited to our nearby house party with our neighbors, primarily older teenage kids. My mother was concerned about me attending the party since I would be one of the youngest children there. However, she took comfort in the fact that I was attending with my brother, who would watch out for my safety. My mother said, *"Have fun tonight at the party, and you guys, be careful."*

This event ended up dramatically shifting my young child's life. My brother and I arrived at the party, which was a mix of adults and many neighborhood teenagers. People enjoyed the sporadic scene and the casual melody effect of the house party. According to my community neighbors, I was a younger form of my older brother, so I passed the 'likable' screening during the house party and continued partying as they did for fun. I enjoyed this new experience, which included loud music and wild teenagers dancing while loving the beautiful weather. This was a young kid's dream that entailed an awesome hip-hop party experience which was like a scene from a *B.E.T. video.*

According to my father, the owner of the house was a gun-happy policeman. He would use his gun sporadically for uncalled reasons on citizens for innocent offenses. At this time, Black and white police officers would shame innocent individual citizens unjustly. Power ego had a huge effect on many police officers. I felt a little weird at the party, being too young, but I was fine because my older brother was chaperoning me. A young girl was dancing with a guy who shockingly touched her inappropriately. The girl's boyfriend was a famous rapper at the time considered a *thug²*.

The rapper noticed a man making sexual and touchy gestures to his girlfriend and began angrily collecting his friends. The entire party of teenagers had consumed lots of alcohol except me because I was too young. Perhaps the effect of drinking alcohol can potentially be negatively dangerous, but the angry people were all drunk and inebriated. The jovial party scene quickly shifted, and two groups of men began arguing loudly, eventually erupting into physical altercation. People were fist-fighting and throwing chairs in the streets. The chaotic scene was amplified by crying and yelling.

I was in the middle of all the commotion when suddenly, I heard a loud gun sound: Boom! Directly after the blast, I heard the sound of a body falling to the ground. Luckily, I was away from the line of fire, but my heart was racing, and my young brain was unable to make sense of the traumatic event I was witnessing. I was crying and emotionally frantic about what had happened. The victim of the fatal gunshot wound was a young teenager who I grew up with and idolized. After this devastating occurrence, I immediately found out who shot him; it was the gun-stoking policeman who owned the house. My older brother, Jamel, was next to the policeman when he shot the teen. After this shooting, my brother rushed me home, and I went to bed in a state of fear and panic.

Next week, the entire community mourned the loss of a young, bright teenage boy. I remember this traumatic event with keen clarity. Nothing happened to the policeman, and they covered up the situation as if he had never committed a criminal murder offense. Regrettably, the police united with each other and kept the incident quiet. After this disturbing event, my family moved to a safe neighborhood in Virginia

---

² My use of the word *thug* is not based on a person's skin color, but their rude actions that negatively affected the community, as this word is usually stigmatized by society.

where my father grew up. We were able to live a calm life, and I was able to get back to normalcy. My best friend, Jamel Smiley, was a little upset about our move to Virginia, but I visited him over the years, and he adjusted overtime with my departure.

This shooting altered my position on the police. Their job is to make communities safe, not hurt us. Even though much of their power is misconstrued, we need not manipulate the cops and should deal with them with constructive reasoning. Let's join forces, regardless of your occupation. In my opinion, we are all equal with purity in our souls. It's time to unite.

Life Lesson #1

Your life and your children's lives are filled with ups and downs. Enjoy it and embrace it. Having to struggle as a youth will help you tackle problems as an adult. Basketball was my sport of choice; you may have a different habit or constructive activity that you enjoy. Our goal is to practice intently and consistently, and these actions will build us up. Stay strong no matter what takes place in life. If you have children, raise them on your ideal of a dream goal. Children are gifts from God. Kids are too young to understand most things, but they mirror their parents and copy their mannerisms, so be careful. Parents should mirror servant leadership to their children to allow them to thrive. Make sure the mirror doesn't crack because kids can't *see you correctly*, meaning your behavior is societally bad, and your actions have a *racial mindset*. I observed this reality unfolding as a youth. Don't forget to uplift other human beings' weaknesses to strengthen them and instill love in your heart, not hate. Your love is a gift to this world. Understand lynching, slavery, cruel racism, and segregation policies are equal occurrences in our society. By this analysis, Black people fear police officers and vice versa. May God bless our youth and make them more righteous; may God unite all human beings with love.

CHAPTER 2

"Heart is what separates the good from the great."
— Michael Jordan.

Moving to the south, we lived in Hampton, Virginia, which was beautifully scenic and featured many beaches with picturesque waterfronts. My mother adjusted her career and began working as a high-paid educational consultant and would travel to many Asian countries. I built a close relationship with two kids in my neighborhood named James Harris and Marc Bacote. They lived on my block and loved basketball and sporting events just as much as I did—a close triad friendship formed between us, with basketball as our commonality. We primarily played sports together every day. I was focused on building strength for sports I played during my adolescent and teen years. My discipline trickled into my schoolwork, and I got high grades. I was in advanced placement classes at a public high school and enjoyed intellectual pursuits.

I was a cocky Black NY kid with stylish confidence and a little too arrogant. As a middle school eighth grader, I played at the J.V. High School level since I was exceptionally good at the sport. I assumed I would play at the same school for my high school career but my plan was somewhat derailed. My brother had a fallout with the head coach, so I decided to transfer to a nearby high school who had just hired a new basketball coach, Mike Tallon. He used to be a women's basketball coach of a team that went to the state championship game. He also coached an exceptional athlete that became as a successful W.N.B.A. player. His character appealed to me and we spent a lot of quality time together. We advanced to the state championships during our high school basketball season but lost to another team. I led the team as a point guard player. Being a star athlete in high school paved the way for me to act superior to my classmates. I embraced a persona of cockiness, confidence, and egotism.

In middle school, I played in a youth basketball program and met an incredible player, Marseilles Brown. As basketball middle school teammates, we won our games easily. Even though we were on different high school teams, we would spend time together hanging out and playing video games. I would always challenge him in basketball since I knew he could help me improve since he was exceptionally talented. His movements with the ball that he systematically worked on perfecting would enhance my defensive skills. During my high school experience, I would prepare intensely for our basketball games against Marseilles, who was leading his team. This healthy competition was key in both of us getting recruited since colleges and universities would watch the games. We both went to a Division I university on basketball scholarships and remained friends later.

As I reflect on my past, I see several incidents that could have dramatically altered a young child's life. Living close to rough New York City neighborhoods and witnessing a knife fight and murder definitely impacted me as a young child. Most children do not participate in protesting social injustices such as the killing of a Black man. Should I have received therapy as a child? Did this trauma negatively affect me? While everyone's situation is different, the simple answer to both questions for me is: No. I found strength and increased my resiliency from these events. I also had a powerful support system from a tight-knit family. As strange as it might sound, I appreciate both the positive and negative experiences that occurred in my childhood. Overall, my life was pretty simple growing up, but certain events altered how I viewed life's fragility. Regardless of who you are, critical life events can change your state both positively and negatively and affect your viewpoint and perspective on life.

How can our communities be humanly, righteously, and virtuously developed? Is there a single person to blame for the state of some communities? Are we responsible for how we develop and are characterized, often based on our living situations and zip codes? We all need to own the goal of creating a pluralistic view of humanity without a bias. We must implement a safe feeling towards others, support the development of all youth, and embrace success regardless of our environment. Let's cultivate **group optimism** one person at a time and empower resiliency in our youth. In today's modern world, it's time to focus on social values that uplift the community to the highest state using digital technology and social media.

We need to spend quality time physically with others to create positive beliefs and attitudes. Social media can connect us to groups that advance a *community-building* mindset. Of course, there will be conflicting points of view since we are all humans with different lived experiences. However, becoming a **servant leader**[3] can allow for greater dialogue and understanding among diverse groups. Allow community-building to become a daily practice. Witnessing the murder of a teenager at a young age could have negatively changed my life forever. However,

---

[3] Servant Leadership: known by a famous writer as leading a group with the heart and having other people's concerns and opinions at the forefront.

strong willpower and resiliency allowed me to successfully kept my life moving forward. And you can too.

ATHLETIC ARROGANCE

After successfully playing basketball in high school, I was recruited by many colleges offering basketball scholarships. I decided to attend a Division 1 university in the state of Maryland, and I lived on campus during my freshman year. I had two roommates, Ernest and Kenny, who were also on the basketball team. They served as small forward and centered, whereas I had a more point guard role. We spent much time together at practices and in our dorm room. Our games were intense since it was a mid-level Division 1 university. I lived a standard scholarship athlete life. My dorm room served as the central hub for most of my activities; I would complete workouts, hang with my roommates, and concentrate on schoolwork there.

Building my physical ability and fortitude was my mission, but my character and behavior were indecent and outlandish. Often, I would attend college parties and behave inappropriately toward other students. I would argue with my teammates during basketball practice or travel during our away games. I had a close relationship with the assistant basketball coaches, but the head coach had a problem with me because I would not listen to others. After committing a lot of drama and agony, the coaches made a tough decision and took my scholarship away; I returned home confused and depressed. As I tried to figure out the next steps of my life, I enrolled in a small chiropractor college in Georgia. However, I soon released that this was a mismatch for me and left quickly as I was not suitable for this type of college. Facing another setback, my depression and irritability increased.

Losing my basketball scholarship gave me the opportunity to take time to reflect. I gathered lesson from my time in Maryland and became a bit more reflective and humble. I was able to continue my education and play basketball at a small college in my hometown in Virginia. Even though I was making positive steps to turn my situation around, losing my basketball continued to sadden me. I had worked towards earning a scholarship since high school youth, and I could have prevented this from happening if my character and behavior were different. My athletic and academic abilities were never in question. If only I had maintained a positive character instead of what I displayed to the coaches and my teammates. I missed my Division I basketball scholarship opportunity and realized it was time to change my behavior.

As my original plan of playing D1-level basketball derailed, a new chapter of my life began where I least expected. Returning home, I started working at a local telecommunications company and balancing work and academic life. One of my coworkers was a beautiful young woman named Apryl McDowell, who was also enrolled at an H.B.C.U. in our area. During breaks at work, we began conversing, and I found myself always anxious to talk to her. One time, I overheard her speaking a foreign language to my friend, James Harris. She used to live in Japan and picked up the Asian language. I commented, *"That's awesome! You speak Japanese. I'll make a deal: for you to teach me this new language, I'll fitness train you. Deal?"* She agreed to exchange services, but my real intention was to get closer to her. Ironically enough, Apryl was the catalyst that helped me turn my life around.

Apryl wasn't Muslim at the time, but she was attracted to Islamic-minded individuals in college. She was not really into dating in college, as she was focused on academic studies and campus activities. She worked hard to achieve high grades and was also on the band dance team. I was fortunate to meet her best friend and got to know her a bit during a deep conversation. After our talk, she gave Apryl her seal of approval, *"Omari…. I really like him a lot."* I knew Apryl would be a special person in my life, but this gave me the extra confirmation I needed. Apparently, the same was true for Apryl. She hadn't been drawn to any of the men she had met until her best friend approved of me. In my estimation, she possessed all the qualities I desired in a mate; she was highly intelligent yet bubbly and funny at times. She was majoring in Computer Science and was in excellent exercise shape as a member of the dance crew that performed with the college football band. Our relationship developed, and we became a couple. The two of us became inseparable; our lives consisted of going to college and working all the time.

Life Lesson #2

Egotism can be a personality sickness. Through faith, you can make it healthy by showing others your caring support and praying for God to erase your flaws. After we lose something we value - like my love for playing basketball at a Division 1 school – we can fall into a state of depression. We can mitigate such negativity by making positive adjustments and rejecting harmful character traits or dispositions that are detrimental to our success. In my journey, it was the religion of Islam that helped establish my humility and changed my arrogance. The same concept applies to you. Be intentional in your pursuit of perfection; actively work on changing your negative qualities and embracing positivity.

Figure 1 The Grey family

Figure 1 Family Grey

Figure 2 Childhood friends

CHAPTER 3

"Talent is God-given. Be humble. Fame is man-given. Be grateful. Conceit is self-given. Be careful."

— John Wooden

My first introduction to the religion of Islam was through a friend, Yusef Jamaludeen. We met in a youth basketball team in Hampton, Virginia, and we connected on our mutual love of the sport. In high school, his mannerisms and behaviors were different from that of typical teenagers. He avoided many activities that I participated in due to his religious beliefs. Still, we stayed close friends during our college days. He was extremely funny, and I enjoyed being around him as he would always make me laugh.

After getting kicked off of the D1 college basketball team, I became more humble and reflective about life. As my current situation was a result of negative character traits I had, I knew I needed to make major changes in my life. My heart longed for a system that would allow for intense character development. I admired how Yusef had not gotten caught up in destructive activities in college. Was it his religion that helped him avoid wild college antics? How was he able to resist the temptations of reckless youth behavior? Our friendship began to shift as my interest in his faith grew. Slowly, I started to adopt the principles and practices of the religion they resonated strongly with me.

The more I leaned into this new way of life, the more humble I became. I finally entered into the fold of Islam by publicly stating the *shahada*, the Muslim profession of faith, that I believed that there was only one God. Praise God; God is great. After saying these words, my previous wrongdoings were erased – one of the happiest moments of my life. My conversion created a new Omari Grey. Islam taught me how to build my character. There was no reason to change my first name, which originates from the Swahili[4] language. Even though my mother had given me this name, it still enabled me to be distinguished as a Muslim. It was as if this was a Godly plan from birth, and I was merely returning to my true nature. Part of my testimony of faith also included declaring my belief in a final messenger, Prophet Muhammad (may peace be upon him). He was a righteous, sincere person whom I had to strive to emulate. As I tried to embrace his ways, I began reading books about his life and narrations. One of the sayings that stood out to me was: **there is no beauty better than intellect**. After reading this, my pursuit of knowledge increased, and I began reading more and listening to podcasts.

After my conversion to Islam, I realized I needed to be married, as casual dating is not allowed. Apryl developed an interest in the faith and converted to being a Muslim as well. After she took her religious testimony, she changed somewhat. Instead of being infatuated with me, her Islamic religion became her top priority. Immediately she began following the religion's rules and did her best to stick to Islamic truths. She changed her name to *Sakinah*, an Arabic word meaning serenity and

---

[4] The Swahili culture was connected to the Arab people in the nineteenth century. Being close to East Africa and visiting, the Swahili's changed their religion to Islam after being closely connected to the Arabs because of a trade agreement.

tranquility. To me, this was the perfect name for her as she embodied these traits.

After her conversion, I asked Sakinah to marry me, and she accepted my proposal. I was living with a close friend name James Harris at the time. He graciously decided to leave our townhouse so we could start our journey as newlyweds. At this point, my life was very calm and relaxing as I concentrated on finishing college and obtaining my bachelor's degree. I was happily married to an amazing woman. We would engage in discussions about Islamic principles both at work and in our townhouse. Islam became our main focus. I was also playing Division III college basketball which was less intense and more enjoyable for me. I felt at ease and peaceful due to my religion.

At first, my routine was working full-time while also attending classes and basketball practices. Sakina would cheer me on at my games, and we continued working at the telecommunications company. I was thoroughly infatuated with my wife and tried to treat her in the best manner possible. Being an ideal husband and growing in faith, I decided to leave the basketball team to concentrate on my religious practice and wife. I continued to enjoy playing basketball for fun, but my academic studies, family life, and religion took priority.

I finally finished all my degree requirements and was excited to celebrate the completion of this long journey with my family. From losing my basketball scholarship and briefly attending school in Georgia to finally graduating, this was quite an accomplishment for me. Education is extremely important as it unlocks opportunities. My family attended my graduation to support me. During the commencement, I couldn't hold in my gratitude that God had brought me to the end of this journey and had transformed my life. I briefly interrupted one of the professors who was speaking and began loudly shouting *Allahu Akbar*, which means "God is great" and is used to acknowledge special occasions. The Muslims at my graduation joined me, and we chanted in unison. Even though I now feel that was inappropriate, I was proud (maybe even a bit fanatical) to be considered a Muslim.

After receiving my college degree, I continued to work as normal. I began to attend the nearby Islamic center regularly and spent time with the brothers I met there, who were primarily from Egypt. I interacted with many other cultures also, including Ghanaians, Pakistanis, and Sudanese people. It was a bit challenging to communicate with some of the religious leaders due to the language barrier. I was excited to learn Arabic to understand the Holy Quran, the book which God has revealed in this language. Sakinah and I became troubled that we could not understand Arabic. I was always intrigued by different languages and chose to study Spanish in college. I chose this language because my mother's best friend, Vicky Septh, spoke Spanish, and she was lovely and kind to me. However, now I want to read the Holy Quran and understand prayers and other rituals conducted in Arabic.

Sakinah and I attempted to take classes locally, but we failed to make any significant progress. Slowly the idea of living abroad took root as we contemplated how committed we were to make a drastic change. Leaving the U.S. for the Middle East seemed a bit extreme, but it was the type of sacrifice that would allow us to reach our goals truly or, at the very least, improve our Arabic. I became exceedingly hungry to grow in my religious knowledge. After much thought, we decided that it was time to leave America.

Life Lesson #3

When I converted to Islam, my entire way of life changed. I call this the *human metamorphosis*. Converting to Islam transformed my philosophy on life and broadened my love for all human beings. Your path might be different but seek to make changes in your life that align you with true joy and head. Alter anything that makes you joyfully happy and has a well-thought-out vision. Allow people to enjoy their beliefs because religions to God make you feel significant, which is important. This significance is a human need. My life has changed in a new direction. Now your turn to change. Just make it happen, and don't look back. Sacrifice instilled determination like me leaving the U.S. How are you creating a new you? What are you *mentally converting*?

Figure 3 Basketball team

Figure 4 Young Omari

Figure 5 Brother, father, and Omari

PART II

Overseas Life

CHAPTER 4

CAPITALIZE POVERTY

After I converted, I asked myself often: "Who is Omari Grey? What is his life mission?" I had obtained my bachelor's degree and was ready for the next chapter of my life. One of the ideas swarming around in my mind was working as a teacher overseas. Having a global mentality and gaining different perspectives on how others live can help build compassion with other people. As one travels, one becomes comfortable dealing with different mindsets and grows compassionate toward others. My wife and I applied for overseas teaching jobs to expand our horizons. One of the jobs we found was in Taiwan, China. When investigating this possibility, we were shamefully told that this institution did not hire people of color.

I would frequent the local masjid (Islamic religious center) as I lived very close to it. Religious traditions give people solace and comfort, which is what Islam offers to me. I did my utmost to obtain a high level of piety but often fell short of reaching the spiritual goals I set for myself. Each day, I attempted to wake up early and pray *Fajr*, the Islamic morning prayer, and I was happy when I succeeded.

I concentrated daily on improving my spirituality. There was much to learn as everything was new for me. I searched for religious scholars I could relate to for guidance and focused on those I thought embodied spiritual success. One such individual was Sheikh Hamza Yusuf, a famous Islamic scholar who spent time in Yemen and lived with other spiritually-connected individuals. Sakinah and I heard one of his lectures on religion and got excited. Sheikh Hamza Yusef once said: *"People say to you, 'you've changed,' or something like that; well, I hope, for the sake of God, that you have changed because I don't want to be the same person all my life. I want to be growing, expand, and change. Animate things change, but inanimate things don't change because dead things don't change. The heart should be alive, changing, moving, and growing its knowledge. The heart should be expanding."* I wanted to change, and in my opinion, the only way to accomplish that was by leaving the U.S.

Many American Muslims travel internationally to increase their spirituality and develop firm beliefs. My goal for traveling to the Middle East was to increase my spirituality by being in a country populated by individuals who lived the Islamic lifestyle from birth. As I looked at Sheikh Hamza Yusuf as a model of compassion and wisdom, I contemplated following in his footsteps and moving to Yemen. After seeing other people's light develop in Yemen, I decided that this was the country I wanted to visit. It was time to experience other countries, different personalities, languages, and Arab cultures.

My wife felt the same way and found an American-based school in Yemen. Getting a school teaching job in Yemen was relatively easy for American citizens. We quickly bought our plane tickets and began setting up our arrangements. My parents were shocked that we were going to Yemen, as it was portrayed in the news as an unsafe environment. Yemen was often painted with a negative image. Although Yemen has a lot of oil and gas resources and agriculturally productive land, it remains one of the poorest countries in the world. More than 80 percent of the population lives in poverty.

We departed the U.S. and flew with our close friends, Toi and Terry, who were headed to Kuwait. Upon arriving in Yemen, we experienced culture shock. Many things were different than what we were accustomed to from growing up in the U.S. It was scary at first, but we eventually adjusted as we experienced the warmness of the local people. One of the first things that caught us off guard was the bathrooms. Unless there was an American-style toilet, most restrooms simply had holes in the floor to use. To get around, we used taxis as our transportation; the taxi cab drivers were routinely amazed to meet us. Seeing practicing young American Muslims was unfamiliar to most; we were not what they expected to pick up in their taxis.

We struggled financially but did our best to make do with what we had. We got paid $600US a month, which was triple the number that other teachers made since we were American citizens. Yemeni food was also very different; I didn't eat much of it but enjoyed it. We lived off of a diet of basic American food. My wife would cook eggs and hot dogs that I found at the store. I created a humorous song, "hot dogs and French fries, that's all right with me." to bring us happiness in the environment we had chosen to live in. We often visited the Yemeni marketplace and enjoyed different cultural events and festivities. Sadly, many Yemeni people were zombied out by a drug called Khat[5].

We spent a lot of time with the locals, who were sincere, warm, and compassionate. We were invited into their homes and enjoyed their hospitality and kindness. We lived in a great house where diplomats stayed. We dealt with some minor health issues during our time in

---

[5] Khat consumption induces mild euphoria and excitement, similar to that conferred by strong coffee as a stimulant drug. Individuals become very talkative under the influence of the plant.

Yemen. I had a severe case of diarrhea due to the Yemeni water I accidentally drank for a while. Even though our illnesses existed, we dealt with them and comfortably moved on with our lives. During this time, we were blessed with our first pregnancy. Her first trimester was difficult as she battled with morning sickness. Once, we rode a bus for transportation, and Sakinah began throwing up on people's laps.

We both worked at an American school owned by an African-American woman who served as the principal and a Yemeni man. Strangely enough, we were the only Americans who worked at the school. After we began working there, I realized that the principal was a fraud and would lie about many unnecessary things. For example, she told my wife her weave was her real hair, even though my wife could clearly tell it was not her real hair. She also said she held seven college degrees, which I doubted was possible. She claimed she was British, even though she spoke with an American accent at times. We slowly began to notice that the principal was incorporating fraudulent behavior. She was taking advantage of the people in this developing country. I saw through her from the beginning. However, the Yemeni people were convinced she was kind and sweet.

As we continued to live and work in Yemen, we began to experience conflict with the principal of the American school. We became disillusioned by the principal, and I was ready to leave Yemen but could not since the school had our passports. It all came to a head one day. I had complained about the school lowering our wages. The principal started causing problems with other teachers about our high payment even though it was a U.S small amount. After teaching class one day, Sakinah and I got called into a meeting by the school owners. I figured it was about my complaint, but I didn't understand why they had also requested other teachers to be present. After walking into the school, my wife and I met the principal and the other teachers in the conference room.

At the meeting, we heard other shocking statements by the principal. My wife had decided to cover her face, which is called a *niqab*, due to wanting to increase her commitment to her faith. The principal claimed that I had abused and hit my wife in the face, which is why she decided to be veiled. The principal said, *"You veiled and covered yourself because you had a black eye!"* She also accused me of pushing my wife down the stairs causing her to miscarry — a straight lie. Sakinah started crying loudly at the principal's accusations, and I tried to calm her down. She could not understand how a Muslim person could lie so easily. As a new Muslim, Sakinah knew that lying and slander were unlawful for Muslims.

The principal's lies were not shocking to me because I had quickly realized who the principal was as a person, no matter her religion. After hearing the principal's words, I quickly snatched our passports that were being held at the school and ran. Holding my wife's hand, we dashed towards the school's gate, praying it was unlocked. We heard the principal tell the security guards on a walkie-talkie to lock the doors, but we luckily ran outside the school just in time. We were frantic, in a foreign country with little funds, and had nearly escaped from our previous employer. Jobless and alone, we picked up the phone in desperation and frantically called home with what little money we had from our teaching pay. We quickly spent all of our money as international phone calls were very expensive at the time.

I decided to contact the embassy, hoping to get their needed help. After this incident, we called some friends who were living in Kuwait and told them we had to leave this country quickly. They helped us leave Yemen and begin a new chapter in Kuwait. It was a dramatic end to our first overseas adventure. I didn't leave because of the Yemeni people; the locals were beautiful with amazing character. The sole reason was that this African-American principal took advantage of Yemen's poor people. I am blessed to be a United States citizen, and I believe I should use this privilege to aid the poor in other countries with kindheartedness, not use them like this lady was.

Life Lesson #4

I lived in Middle Eastern countries for ten years and visited Qatar, Turkey, and Egypt. Our goal was to learn how to speak the Arabic language, but there was so much more we gained from our overseas experience. Visiting developing countries, we saw a plethora of trauma and community mayhem which causes psyche damage for poor individuals. After I was in a traumatic car accident and became a crippled state, my life flipped into a type of physical weakness. I learned firsthand how people in need and pain require our good actions and care. It's not just an economical deficiency but any human weakness. Solution: Help others. Secondly, instill practical minimalism, which means avoiding unnecessary things in life. Less is more.

Figure 6 Sanaa, Yemen

Figure 7 Old City Sanaa Yemen

Figure 8 Traditional clothing

CHAPTER 5

OIL-RICH COUNTRY

After leaving Yemen, we settled in Kuwait. This small country, located off the Persian Gulf near Iraq, is about 20% of the size of the United States. It has the highest gross domestic product (GDP) of oil percentage among the Organization of the Petroleum Exporting Countries (OPEC) nations, so most locals live very comfortably. They accept workers from across the Middle East who were interested in working in their country. Kuwait was an extremely small version of the United States, so I could easily explore the entire country.

I did not have a teaching certification at the time. However, because Osama Bin Laden was going to war with Kuwait, I easily found a math teaching job at a British school. Sakinah was dealing with a rough pregnancy which often caused her to be physically sick. Her close friend, Toi Warren, told us to come to stay with them and that she would help with her pregnancy. I worked at a British school first, then was able to work at an American school as a math teacher. I was treated so kindly by the Kuwaiti people as an American. The hospitality I received was overwhelming. For me, this type of treatment felt strange. Why did I receive more respect from the Kuwaiti people than my fellow citizens in America?

I loved my experience in Kuwait and also enjoyed coaching basketball at a recreational league. As everyone was frantically leaving Kuwait due to the war, we were entering the country. We were young twenty-year-old Americans who were not scared of living in countries struck with war, so we stayed in Kuwait. Initially, I worked just as a math teacher. After becoming a certified fitness trainer at this well-known gym and a basketball coach at a club, it made sense to become a physical education teacher at the school. I was respected by students and staff members and touched many of their lives.

Another American teacher once got into an argument with a staff member. After their exchange, I walked with the American teacher and shared my perspective with him so that he could change his mindset. Eventually, he calmed down and relaxed. This became a routine for me, and I easily conversed with people in Kuwait and every part of the globe. Living overseas requires us to broaden our ways of thinking. We should adjust to unfamiliar cultures and understand their ways of thinking, and truly grow from our travels.

We ended up living in Kuwait for ten years. I began fitness training at a local gym, and some of my clients were extremely rich. After getting into a car accident, one of my clients, a Kuwaiti prince, allowed me to select one of his many cars from his huge driveway to use. Students and staff also respected me tremendously, and I would give others a great deal of advice. Kuwait was a country they would greet each other and say, "how are you?" as an Arabic slang translated word: *shlonak*. I used to love to say this every day. I stayed in Kuwait the longest out of all the foreign countries I lived in for a reason. This country economically was wealthy, and the people were the same religion as me. There were so many American and British people because of the hospitality and reverence the Kuwaitis gave to foreign Westerners. A lesson can be taken from this: treat others with nobility, and they will flock to you, just like the Westerners did to Kuwait.

A good friend of mine that I went to high school with in Virginia was also living in Kuwait at the time. When we were in high school, I used to go over basketball drills and spend time hanging out with him. Nassir and I had similar stories of finding Islam, and it was a gift that we were able to share time in Kuwait together. His first name was Marty Francisco, and he had a friend in college who was a practicing Muslim. This friend recommended that Nassir read the Autobiography of Malcolm X. This book detailed the life of Malcolm X, an African-American Muslim Minister who was an important activist in the Civil Rights movement[6]. Nassir was excelling academically in college, so adding another book to read was not a real concern. One day, Nassir went to the campus bookstore and saw his Muslim friend, who told him the Malcolm X book was on sale. After hearing this, Nassir bought the book and read it. He was captivated by the story of a man who went from being imprisoned and pimping women into a huge dignified celebrity respected by everyone in the world.

Nassir didn't realize how a man's whole life could be changed by one book. He quickly devoured the book's content, unable to put it down. He was intrigued to find out how a religion transforms a person from this extremely low state to a high state. He then began reading the Holy Quran, which shifted his beliefs. Gradually, he stopped going out and engaging in negative substances. After a lot of contemplation, he decided to convert to Islam. During the summer, he went to a local religious center. The first person he saw inside the door was me, after not seeing each other for some years.

---

[6] Civil Rights: A movement started to abolish racial segregation and racism against "colored people.

I told Nassir about opportunities that existed at my Kuwaiti school to become a counselor. He agreed and is still happily living there. Spending quality time together and discussing philosophical viewpoints became our routine in Kuwait. I believe accepting other cultures is a strategy for community building, and he felt the same. After I left Kuwait, we stayed in contact with each other. Reflecting on Nassir's conversion, I am aware of the impact books can have on a person. They can give you a better perspective, help you build influence, and have a successful life.

COMPASSIONATE LEADERSHIP

After attending a religious conference during a brief visit to the U.S., I met a mid-western American older gentleman that inspired me with his spirituality and great character. He taught us how to implement Islam in our hearts. He lived in Amman, Jordan, with many disciples he was helping to rejuvenate their spirituality. I decided to spend time in Jordon to grow my faith further. During my stay in Amman, I connected with many people who visited from countries worldwide, including Australia, Canada, America, Egypt, Sweden, South Africa, and Somalia.

My time in Amman made me reflect on how we connect with others of different nationalities. I spent a great deal of time with them at the basketball park, in religious lessons, and eating meals in their home. I learned a lot from this experience. Our relationships stood on one common goal dictated by this American spiritual leader. Even at the gym and while playing basketball on the court, I would try to exhibit great character with everyone seeking fitness and sports skills. While playing at the park with the men, I realized they didn't have the skills

I had, as I had gained basketball skills from a lifetime of playing. I did my best to support and coach them as we played.

Walking at a quick pace toward the mountains with the spiritual leader became a daily form of exercise. The religious scholar convinced me to train and exercise all the men, so I did. He stressed that exercise is extremely important since it cures diseases and increases productivity. This spiritual guide selected me to lead exercises with his people and would talk to me often during our walking exercises on the hill. During our time together, I would carefully observe his excellent character and behavior with anyone who saw him. Our walks, religious ceremonies, and thoughtful conversation made it clear how to emulate the Prophet Muhammad (may peace be onto him).

I have been blessed to have traveled to many foreign countries. However, my experience in Amman was completely transformative and clarified my life's goal. My mission was to become a compassionate leader by emulating the Prophet's character, mindset, words, and, most importantly, his sympathy. After staying in Amman, I focused on improving my character: changing how I was and erasing ugly traits (malice, hatred, envy, arrogance, etc.), making God my main desire. I realized the importance of one's *slavehood* to God and overcoming the biggest obstacle, our ego.

My spiritual guide taught us how to implement the religious law in the Islamic book and how to apply it to life. He was our spiritual coach, and I was the fitness coach for the people in his community. I'll never forget the great relationship I built with many people from many countries when I lived in Amman. After spending some years overseas, it was finally time to return home to America. My experience living abroad helped me formulate the idea of an enriched global community. Living in the Middle East, in total, helped my Islamic faith and built my character.

Life Lesson #5

I lived in Middle Eastern countries for ten years and visited Qatar, Turkey, and Egypt. We live with people and places that transform our lives. For me, Amman, Jordan transformed me significantly. For you, the same applies, except you have to use critical thinking in two ways:

1. Question your assumptions (especially when the stakes are high). Ask yourself, "what is the best way forward?"
2. Poke at the logic; when evaluating arguments, consider if the situation builds on itself to produce a sound conclusion.

This critical thinking strategy made me live in the world's best country, Jordan. My spiritual goal was accomplished and a success. Think about your future goals and desired achievements in the present moment and praise God.

Figure 9 Omari with firstborn son

Figure 10 Omari in Amman, Jordan

Figure 11 Omari in Jordan

PART III

Jack of All Trades

CHAPTER 6

FITNESS EXCELLED FAITH

After living overseas, we returned to the U.S. and decided to live in Northern Virginia. I started working as a math teacher at a private Islamic school. I enjoyed belonging to a community as the school's principal was the wife of the religious community leader of the Islamic center. I loved that my work life and religious life were intertwined daily. My days were extremely busy. After morning prayer, I would coach fitness exercises to a group of Muslim men at a local gym. This soon became a routine that I did on most days.

Among my clients were friends that belonged to a Muslim rap group called Native Deen. The musicians started a streaming channel station called Deen T.V.[7] Since they worked out with us, the idea came to create a fitness show called The Body's Rights show. This name came from the gym I owned in Amman, which I derived from a saying of the Prophet Muhammad (may God give him peace). The *Hadith*, or authentic narrations, said that the body has the rights over you. I would lead the others as a head coach during the sessions

---

[7] DeenTV is the Muslim community's first online channel streaming the best halal entertainment 24/7 to your computer, tablet, mobile phone, and a streaming device.

and structure the exercise. The program was easy because most of the men were in great physical shape. The two loves of my life were physical exercise and religious stability, which this television program provided to me.

We would complete our fitness routines at a gym and a local high school football field. I created an intense training program to ensure they achieved optimal fitness results. At the end of the workout, we would pray to God in unison. I truly enjoyed this time; combining fitness with my faith allowed me to grow in both. Thank God. Our friendship went beyond working out, and I continued to have a close connection with them for many years.

After physically training, exercising in a group, and traveling overseas, I was fortunate enough to get on the cover of the famous Men's Health magazine in 2015 as an "Ultimate Men's Health Guy" along with other men. Since this magazine cover was shot in New York, I had a chance to visit my extended family. This was my chance to shine; I used this opportunity to spotlight important issues and raise awareness. During my talk with the Men's Health magazine, I discussed traveling overseas to Gaza, visiting a Palestinian refugee camp, and observing the suffering in this community. This experience made me rethink my existence and shifted my mental paradigm toward what efforts I could do to build humanity. Visiting Palestine, I understood, as an African American, what apartheid looks and feels like.

ARABIC QURAN HEALING

I also worked for an Arabic language company that taught customers how to read the Quran. After being one of their clients, I became an employee of Fawakih Institute and loved the camaraderie and unison built within this company. While working there, an instructor from

New York named Ismail Ibn Ali, Mariam Khan, and I started the Family Life Initiative. I was responsible for doing outreach and recruitment. To promote this new company, I would visit college campuses, attend Islamic conferences across America, and begin programs to motivate people to read the Quran. I would challenge college students and Fawakih customers not to be complacent in life.

The company's Executive Director was Saif Omar, with whom I had a close relationship. We would discuss many topics, including ways to expand the business. I learned how to be a Muslim entrepreneur from Saif. One of Saif Omar's beliefs was: Life was not the same because of learning the Quran. I felt the same way. May God reward Saif and everyone from Fawakih. During my time with Fawakih Institute, I met many Muslim celebrities, and I admired their positive traits and wanted to emulate them. I would also talk often with Saif's brother, Saad Omar. As a convert to Islam, Fawakih Institute helped establish my heart in love for the Quran; my sincerity to God grew with this company. I look forward to being involved with them in the future, God willing. As you seek employment, seek to get involved in a company with similar values and like-minded people. For me, that was a company attached to the Arabic Quran.

I found a good-paying job in Washington, D.C, during my math teaching career. As a former basketball player, I also became a part-time coach for a boys' team at a nearby Y.M.C.A. Living in an upper-middle-class area near the city of Washington, D.C., and being close to my jobs and religious organizations created much stability for me. My family and I would visit people, pray with people at the religious organization, and I would work nearby. My life was filled with struggles, but I had many successes in my career as a fitness trainer. I began training millionaires at their homes. I also did group home training for women and their children. It was a busy life as I carefully planned all aspects of the training sessions. I would develop motivational songs and effective exercise routines.

I also worked for a woodworking company that had millionaire and billionaire clientele. I started as a beginner employee and worked my way up to the company's top. I was the only Black employee and had a great relationship with the other employees. My role changed with the company to that of a consultant; improving employee motivation and increasing productivity was my focus. I worked at the job during the summer when I was on break from my regular teaching job. This company was growing and trying to ignite a learning and continuous improvement culture. After six weeks, my job shifted to a consultant role focused on personal and team growth. I organized a Spartan Race obstacle course to challenge the employees with fitness. I even reached out to nonprofit organizations in Charlottesville, VA, to build a wooden fence. I created a great bonding time, and it was enjoyable. After visiting some farms and understanding how they make a profit, an idea sprouted.

Even though I was fulfilled living in the upper-middle-class suburbs, I was constantly busy and missed a simpler lifestyle. After much debate, we decided to embrace a self-sufficiency lifestyle. Self-sufficiency is being able to supply one's needs without external support and having extreme confidence in one's own resources. While self-sufficiency is a broad lifestyle that can look very different for various people, I knew it was something I wanted for myself and my family. After teaching overseas for a decade and living in the suburbs, it was time to embrace a self-sufficient lifestyle, and farm life was my goal to achieve that.

My family history in America has roots in slavery, a common storyline for many African-Americans. An individual who enslaved my ancestors grew fond of one of the enslaved Black men. He gave this man a portion of land in Virginia which, the way I view it, was given as an apology to our family for the injustice, wrong, and dehumanizing enslavement period. Members of my family had a successful, profitable farm. My family and I moved into an RV close to this land and began developing a productive farm and living a life of self-sufficiency. Sakinah and I had been blessed with many sons and daughters, and we embarked on a journey to become real homesteaders.

This was a very, extremely busy time for me. Working as a math teacher and fitness coach, having homesteader responsibilities on top of that, was exhausting. It was a two-hour drive to D.C. for math teaching from our farm, creating a lot of tiredness and fatigue. I was ready for a change in my life, so I left my teaching job in Washington, D.C. We decided to live in an RV with nine children. Our living structure was small, with us being extremely close to each other daily. Living in an RV was a sacrifice, but I easily overcame it with little discomfort.

I experienced much guilt leaving my teaching job. We went from living in a comfortable suburban home to this extremely small RV. I thought: how can I raise my whole family of eleven people in a recreational vehicle? We stayed at different RV resorts and lived on our land in Virginia for around two years. At first, I felt extremely distraught because I had completely uprooted my family and changed from a comfortable one to one with many challenges. But in the end, I stopped my negative thoughts as I knew this sacrifice would get us close to how we wanted to live our lives long-term— changing my expectations allowed for a better adjustment to living in a small RV. If I didn't expect to live in a large beautiful house, I was fine adjusting to this downgrade. Often having expectations can lead to suffering.

From a teenage New Yorker who loved the city to becoming a real farmer was quite a drastic change. I decided to live life with a limitless way of thinking. Eventually, we moved permanently to live on the inherited land. My family and I would attend organized farmer workshops and gain a plethora of information to help our farm business thrive and succeed. Our farm became a sanctuary for the soul, and we loved hosting events and workshops for people to come. At this time, I became very active in the community and promoted community building. I would often arrange free gatherings with men, women, and kids. My wife disagreed on why I didn't charge more money for the events I was doing. Our finances were struggling; we barely managed to survive comfortably since I quit my teaching job and canceled my fitness coaching position. Our condition was in a bit of a poor state as we lived in an RV and a constructed Yurt. Sakinah wanted me to focus on ensuring my family was more comfortable. I reminded her about our bigger goals instead of the current situation. I told her to shift our minds to the target we wanted to accomplish. I always said: Long-term goals motivate you from short-term failures.

2020 was a unique time for the world as it faced the Covid-19 pandemic. For our organic farm business, this was a plus. Everyone was more conscious about the foods they ate and places they frequented; our farming business safely delivered food to their front door and was thriving. I was becoming a real farmer, although I had other part-time jobs, and felt very happy with our situation. We used to attend a well-organized homestead program run by a couple named Doug and Stacy. They were a wealth of knowledge, and Sakinah and I wanted to emulate this inspiring couple.

Life Lesson #6

Coming back to the U.S., I worked numerous jobs, which made me extremely happy. Your day should begin with a strong sense of happiness too. Joy in your actions will keep you moving comfortably forward, no matter your challenges. Sometimes comfort can become a distraction and may leave us moving away from our goals and not accomplishing anything. Having a busy life caused me to search for a different path and becoming a farmer, which brought me more peace. Farming is a real form of peacefulness to your soul. Engaging with many animals and planting fruits and vegetables has given me tranquility. This new life created new changes. Allow new life changes to positively push your path of success instead of allowing them to overwhelm you. Just work hard on yourself.

Figure 12 Coach Omari

Figure 13 Fitness Coaching

Figure 14 Coach Omari

Figure 15 Family farm life

Figure 16 Spartan Race

Figure 17 Fitness Guru

Figure 18 Our Daughters

Figure 19 Our Sons

CHAPTER 7

"Then indeed, with hardship comes ease. Indeed with hardship comes ease."

— (Quran 94:5-6)

My entire life changed dramatically on June 17th, 2020. Life was very busy with running a successful farm, but I truly had begun to love it. Even though I worked three occupations and was a farm entrepreneur, I just did my best to stay focused on delivering customers their food. It was a routine Wednesday, and I was exhausted from everything I was doing. I delivered some fresh food to our Northern Virginia customers and visited a friend. I headed home, driving our farm vehicle. After this long day, I started to fall asleep at the wheel and accidentally drifted into the opposite lane. Unfortunately, as I moved into the wrong lane, a large tractor-trailer was driving and didn't notice my car until it was too late. My business vehicle ended up colliding head-on with a tractor-trailer.

Due to the accident's severity, my distorted body was quickly airlifted to the nearest emergency room. The trauma to my body was extensive; I had multiple fractures in my skull, ribs, hips, and leg. My lung was punctured, and I had bleeding in my brain. The doctors told Sakinah that I would die soon and that our family should begin preparing for my funeral with a religious leader. Even if my physical condition improved and there was any hope of living, I would remain in a "persistent, vegetative state" for the rest of my life, according to the medical professionals assigned to asset my situation.

My family had to digest this shocking information and didn't know how to handle this situation. As Allah had planned, I was connected to a Muslim doctor who knew me and ensured that I was well cared for at the hospital. Sakinah was determined that I would indeed live. She was persistent and asked the doctor multiple questions about my injury state, suggested ways of naturally healing my body, and stubbornly refused to leave the hospital scene even after being told by doctors to exit. They thought she was somewhat of a crazy person.

Our community surrounded us with loving care. Close Muslim women friends stepped up and allowed my wife to stay in their homes with them. Even a religious leader, Yafees Sarwar, with whom I studied religion in Jordan, arranged a prayer for me through Social Media technology. One of the most touching pieces of support came from an unexpected place, a young male hospital employee. When my mother, wife, and hospital employees left my room to go home, this young man stayed by my side. He is a hafiz, an individual who has memorized the entire Holy Quran, the sacred scripture of Islam. He would read this holy scripture aloud to my tubed-filled, crippled body when everyone else had gone home.

The very next day, the hospital employees came back to work. The decision was to end life support by removing my tubing and allowing me to die with dignity. It was assumed that my time on this earth was up, but my Creator had different plans than what they expected. Suddenly there was a loud sound that came from the hospital devices. The heart device miraculously picked up; I began breathing normally and slowly opened my eyes. The doctors were shocked and amazed; I was one of their first patients to recover from such a traumatic car accident. Not knowing I was alive, my wife frantically joined our hospital group and wanted to understand my coma state. She met with some hospital nurses, and their first question to her was, *"So, what type of music should we play to your husband? He's alive!"* My wife and mother were exceedingly happy and laid beside me the whole day.

Beyond the medical interventions and treatments, the hospital doctors and nurses did not realize that perhaps healing came from another source. Maybe the young hafiz who stayed in my room overnight possibly may have helped me live. I came to learn of this young hafiz and what he did as I had a chance to meet him during my recovery. He told my wife and me at the restaurant one day, and then he drifted off to live his life. The power of prayer works. Prayer talks to God and transforms us.

COMMUNITY HEALING

My car accident caused me to suffer a traumatic brain injury which completely changed my life. I lost my three jobs and could not help support my wife and our nine children. The doctor said it might take me two years or longer to recover and heal. Through a crowdfunding company called LaunchGood, two friends, David Hawa and Sajjad Ahmed, started a digital campaign. May God reward you, brothers! After some time, this call for support got through to many people I knew personally and many I didn't know. Over 15,000 people donated 1.1 Million dollars! Hearing this news, Sakinah said, *"Omari...now I understand why you wanted to help the community, and I see the big long-term picture."* She realized the interconnectedness of human beings; our previous sacrifice for others paved the way for thousands of people to help us during our time of need.

My recovery is a very long process. I spent three months fighting and regaining strength and two months in the intensive care unit. As I prepared to leave the hospital, the doctor recommended some therapists and support groups to help me during my recovery period. I left the hospital in a wheelchair supported by my oldest son, Muhammad, and returned to our farm in Virginia. Muhammad was attending a nearby college, so he lived with us.

Everything shut down in my mind completely due to the car accident. I didn't understand who Omari Grey used to be; my character, charisma, and personality were completely altered. Early one morning, I woke up with an excruciating headache and neck pain for the first time since my car accident. Since I had a memory loss issue, I did not recall the incident, so I didn't understand where my pain was coming from. I found out a newspaper did an article on my traumatic car accident, so I was interested in reading it. I looked online for their article and found some pictures of the SUV I was driving. My vehicle was so totaled that you couldn't recognize the shape of this normal car! It had broken windows, busted tires, and due to the speed of smashing a large truck, my front hood was folded upwards as well as the driving window.

After seeing my torn, broken SUV, I was thrilled to be living again. It was truly a God miracle. I tried to go into the kitchen but remembered that I needed my sons to help me due to my crippled state. After yelling their names out loud, my oldest son, Muhammad, came to assist me. Sitting in my wheelchair and assisted by my son, I rolled up to the kitchen table to eat food. It smelled delicious, and I was impressed that my ten-year-old girl created such a meal with her superb cooking skills. I tried to eat, but I could not properly move my mouth. Also, picking up the knife and fork was difficult due to my arm injury. I was a little frustrated but understood that I would have eating difficulties due to the muscles in my mouth and aphasia[8].

I grew upset with the state of my physical body. This accident became my most humbling experience, especially since I used to be a scholarship athlete, math teacher, and trained fitness coach. My wife noticed my depression and sadness. We sat down together in the living room to watch T.V. She said, *"Realize Omari that you should have died and should not be with us. Praise God. Just pray to God and show some thankfulness except for being upset about your physical state."* After hearing her words, I began reflecting and knew she was correct. Also, the religious, spiritual guide I lived with in Amma sent me a book discussing how human beings have neuroplasticity[9] so I need to have patience. After this conversation with Sakinah, I understood. Thank God.

Often we're upset or sad about events not in our control. This was my situation. There is a justified reason that I'm alive after such a terrible accident, but I couldn't understand why. I thanked my wife again for her wise comment and headed back to my bedroom since fatigue was present in my body. Due to my car accident, I changed my condition. How could I let go of the things I cannot control and react positively? The idea of control is an illusion. God controls things.

POSITIVE PESSIMIST

Adjusting to my new state of being proved to be challenging. Every night I would go to bed and wake up after about four hours due to my brain injury. I tried to erase the feelings I had of being off balance but

---

[8] Definition: loss of ability to understand or express speech caused by brain damage.

[9] The ability of the brain to form and reorganize connections, especially in response to the following injury.

found many difficulties. Often, I would laugh at my children for no reason or get angry and yell at my wife and other friends around our house. I would deeply apologize to her and lay hopelessly in my bed. I felt blessed to be alive after this terrible car accident, but the permanent changes were hard to adjust.

In my home, I stayed in my bedroom by myself, and we had a wooden deck outside the room. I would take my wheelchair outside during the spring and summer months and allow our rabbits to sit on my lap. Living on this large farm and raising many different animals was a form of nature therapy that helped me gain a calm meditative state. My traumatic car accident caused much pain and suffering, but it has help me grow my mental strength and obtain a higher level of well-being. I was comfortable with wanting to look like an idiot in the short term to be successful in the long term. Due to my brain injury, I lost all of my social contacts. I see my family daily but primarily I stay to myself due to laying in my bedroom. Prayer is fundamental in my life; it is a source of guidance, inspiration, pondering, stability, and validation.

ROLE MODELS

As Muslims, we have an annual religious ceremony called *Eid*. We decided to host this event at our farm. I saw a young man who I taught at a religious private school in Northern Virginia, Haseeb Samdani – an American citizen with an Indian nationality. He was with his father who is a certified physician who offers some suggestions for my recovery. Since I had this brain injury, I could not fully remember the time I taught him because he's a college kid now. I told my wife, and then she reminded me and gave me some details. After I heard my wife explain my teaching past, a brain spark plug went off. Now,

I could see how I taught him mathematics in middle school, coached his basketball, and prayed with him often. I was not just his teacher but involved in his life in other positive ways. I realized that having a real role model relationship matters, no matter what background they have in life.

CHARACTER SHAPES YOU

After my car accident, I realized I had to reinvent myself. No longer would I teach mathematics and be a fitness coach. My focus now was on building a strong community; I believe this is my true purpose for living. Looking back at all my life experiences, I see how my past has prepared me. My life has been truly fulfilled. I have experienced many negative situations from witnessing a teen being murdered to my near death car accident and resulting pain. On the other hand, I was blessed to travel and learn about world cultures, get involved with many different people, and simply enjoy a beautiful life as a farmer. Adapting to weaknesses due to my car accident began to expand my mind. I am grateful for the prayers for my healing. In my humble opinion, I believe the prayers have been answered. Thank God.

Life Lesson #7

After my traumatic car accident, I changed my life for the good. This affected my past memories and was a good thing. Now, my life started a new chapter. It begins with the love of God. All I could remember was my community-building strategies for other people. Perhaps this is a sign from God.

After reading this book, I want you to understand that your mind can play tricks on you. Focus your beliefs on the new you of the future and retrain your mind towards community healing and family strength. Establish the answers to these four (4) questions: After reading this book, I want you to understand that your mind can play tricks on you. Focus your beliefs on the new you of the future and retrain your mind towards community healing and family strength. Establish the answers to these four (4) questions:

1. What does community building look like physically, mentally, emotionally, and spiritually?
2. How are you alleviating community pain (starting with yourself)?
3. How are you alleviating others' pain?
4. What does your culture or community value, and how are you achieving that value?

Figure 20 Car Accident

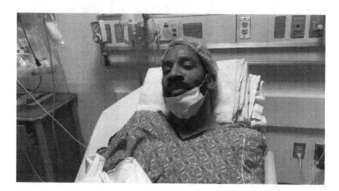

Figure 21 Hospital

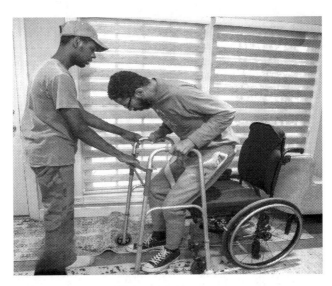

Figure 22 Recovery

EPILOGUE

Growing up, I experienced gun violence and knife fights and lost my Division I basketball scholarship in college. As an adult, I was in a tremendous battle overseas in Yemen and had a traumatic car accident a few years ago. To me, this was God toughening me to help others who are weak. You are the one that narrates your life story. Embrace difficulties and accept your situation; serenity is to enjoy your harmonious relationships with family and friends. Peace is a word meaning no war. Let the war be about improving yourself and eliminating your life disturbances to love other people. Realize Peacefulness Exists.

Thank you for reading this book, take care, and God bless you.

Printed in the United States
by Baker & Taylor Publisher Services